DBT SKILLS WORKBOOK
FOR PARENTS OF TEENS

A Proven Strategy for Understanding and
Parenting Adolescents Who Suffer from
Intense Emotions, Anger, and Anxiety

The Mentor Bucket

TABLE OF CONTENTS

INTRODUCTION

Do you feel tired and exhausted and sometimes regret being a parent? Perhaps your child had once driven you to the point of no return with your emotions, and you had to lash out.

No doubt, parenting can be quite overwhelming, especially when you have a teenager who drives you over the roof by throwing tantrums when you are out together, foot-stomping when a request is denied, having constant meltdowns, being too embarrassed to speak up, and constantly feeling anxious about little things.

The adolescent ages are fraught with many intense emotions that can pose problems for teens who don't know how to manage them. Research has revealed that the ability of a child to cope with the uncertainties of life plays a significant role in their social and academic success, making it important for parents to improve their parenting skills by learning how to tame these emotions and ensure their kids don't lose control of them.

Knowing how to regulate intense emotions involves tolerating difficult feelings such as disappointment and knowing how to react in different social situations. Skills for managing emotions will help a teen be in control of these emotions and act better when they are faced with difficult situations.

I am guessing also that no one told you parenting would be this challenging. Well, many of us weren't told this either, so we just had to learn to be better parents on the job.

As parents, you have an important role in developing and modeling coping skills for your teens, even though many adults are not aware of the basics of emotional intelligence. Unfortunately, many parents have inherited traits of unhealthy coping strategies – including avoidance, yelling, or suppressing emotions – and this puts their children at risk of inheriting the same garbage.

Even skilled parents with high emotional intelligence still find it difficult to parent a teen who exhibits intense emotions. Emotions can be extreme and often unpredictable. They can even turn on a dime.

While managing intense emotions can be difficult, there is hope!

If your child's traits are beginning to escalate into dangerous and aggressive behaviors – such as binging, cutting, throwing things, refusing, threatening, and responding negatively to limits and expectations – you are probably confused and scared already. Don't be scared or feel alone in this situation—many other parents have reported having difficulty managing teenagers with intense emotions, anger, and anxiety.

I was once like you, filled with many questions about how to be in control of one's emotions. I was scared of losing myself until I was introduced to Dialectal Behavioral Therapy (DBT) skills and strategies.

Many times, I have wondered why my child has such intense emotions. It's easy for them to scream because they can't have their way, cry when everyone else is having a good time, look at me with anger on their face when I try correcting them, and see homework as a nightmare. Like you, I finally got to a point where I was scared to tell my child *NO*.

While the behaviors I have described may differ slightly from what your child is experiencing, these are all signs showing that your child suffers from emotional dysregulation. Children with emotional dysregulation tend to react intensely and quickly to circumstances and situations that others don't react to. They will also face a hard time returning to their former, initial state. We can describe children like these as *going from 0 to 100 in split seconds.*

If you've been disturbed by and worried about your child's behaviors and responses to emotions they can't seem to manage in positive ways, parenting with DBT can actually help! It saved me from the nightmare I was in by changing my life and that of my child—for good!

DBT is a skilled therapy structured to help people with intense emotions live better lives. These skills help individuals achieve their goals by reducing behaviors that prevent them from achieving those goals in the first place. With DBT, you can understand and effectively respond to your child's behaviors and emotions.

Parents are taught the idea of emotions, where they come from, and how they function. This helps increase awareness and boost interaction between parents and their children. As parents, you need to learn what makes your teen vulnerable to the intense emotions, triggers, and beliefs that influence their emotional responses. Observe how intense and negative emotions affect your child and how these pose problems. Then you can intervene early and respond with greater acceptance and a good understanding. This allows you to be more effective in helping your child have more control over their emotions and feel better.

DBT teaches you four important skills modules: emotion regulation, mindfulness, interpersonal effectiveness, and distress tolerance. In the modules, you will learn how to help your teens focus their attention, regulate their painful emotions, and deal with distress. You will also find effective strategies for coping with inter-personal conflict.

You can improve your child's behaviors by shaping them with constructive activities, using positive reinforcements and contracts to maintain expectations and limits, and using punishment minimally.

Combining the right information, specific skills, and a nonjudgmental approach will definitely give results. The goal is to live an enjoyable and meaningful life with your family. Even though your family life might differ from your initial vision, DBT provides an increased calm in your life and encourages a well-knit relationship with your child.

Parenting isn't black and white; there are many factors involved in making decisions, so it's not fitting to merely choose one extreme over another. DBT encourages parents to parent from a more balanced perspective, and DBT aims to teach this as well. The word "dialectical" means finding a balance between acceptance and change. This encourages an environment of collaboration and flexibility by teaching your teenagers that while some things are changeable, depending on the circumstances, other things are absolutes.

Rather than downplay the problematic behaviors, or overly focus on normal adolescent development, there is a balance between knowing when a behavior crosses a line and when the behavior is just a typical part of adolescent development. This way, you will know whether to seek professional help or not.

Parents often struggle with maintaining balance in their relationship with their teens as a result of encouraging too much dependence, allowing too much independence, fostering overly close relationships, and not giving enough guidance to their child.

If you are at one end of the spectrum, it's time to find a balance by providing your teen with the right guidance and support while teaching them to take appropriate responsibility. As you step back to increase your child's independence, try to encourage structure at the same time.

Initially, avoiding the black and white, rigid parenting style may be difficult. However, you can do it. With practice, patience, and an altered mindset, you are on track! You will realize that taking a dialectical approach will greatly improve your relationship with your teen.

This book will discuss how you can use some carefully selected DBT strategies and skills to be in more control and live a peaceful life with your teen. If you can help them manage their behaviors and emotions more efficiently, your child will experience a trickle-down effect.

First, I will explain what DBT entails by discussing the modules, the formation of your child's emotions, and the connection between thought, behavior, and feelings.

Also, we'll discuss if emotional dysregulation is just a phase or a real problem in your young one's life and what to do in either case. In this important journey, you must understand your child's emotions, and we'll be discussing their causes, some warning signs, and when to seek help for your child. I'll also present you with effective strategies to help you manage your child's emotions.

Finally, you'll kickstart your new role of being an effective parent. You will learn what it means to be an effective parent, why it is a good way of parenting, how to respond to your child's behaviors and feelings, and various parenting strategies for your child with intense emotions.

My first encounter with DBT was during my years working as a clinician and helping both teenagers and parents battle severe and persistent mental illnesses. Many of the clients I had were battling anxiety, depression, anger, trauma, Post Traumatic Stress Disorder (PTSD), and suicide. With my DBT training, I was able to help people and cater to their needs.

I know there are many people out there battling the same issues. I am writing this book to reach a wider audience, especially people experiencing emotional challenges and who want to set themselves free from the roller coaster of emotions. I designed this workbook to be simple, with complicated terms explained in bits. Inside, you will find exercises to engage in. Ensure you attend to these, as they are a significant part of this process.

So, are you ready to start this exciting journey with me? Flip to the next page, where we'll be discussing DBT and what it entails.

CHAPTER 1:
UNDERSTANDING DBT

Since the start of the 20th century, psychotherapy has witnessed three evolutions: the development of behavioral therapy, which took place in the 1950s, the development of Aaron Beck's cognitive therapy in the 1970s, and the merging of both therapies to present a more contemporary therapy called the cognitive behavioral therapy (CBT). Over the last two decades, there has been an emergence of the "third wave" of cognitive and behavior therapy, which incorporates acceptance and mindfulness techniques.

Dialectical behavior therapy (DBT) is one of the third-wave therapies that have proven to be very effective in treating individuals with Borderline Personality Disorder (BPD) and those with difficulty regulating their emotions. DBT balances cognitive behavioral therapy and humanism using dialectics. Dr. Marsha Linehan developed this therapy in the 1970s after her personal experience with mental illness. DBT was the first psychotherapy to formally incorporate mindfulness into its practice.

What is DBT?

DBT, also known as dialectical behavioral therapy, is a talking therapy treatment performed through a group therapy session and one-on-one talks with individual therapists and a phone coach/therapist. It is based on cognitive behavior therapy but has been adapted to treat people suffering from intense emotions. It also helps struggling individuals identify and change their negative thinking patterns into positive ones.

DBT aims to help individuals:

- Understand and accept their difficult feelings
- Learn skills to help them manage these emotions
- Develop the ability to make positive changes in their lives

The term "Dialectical" in DBT means trying to understand how two opposing things could both be true. For example, the idea of accepting yourself and also changing your behavior may seem contradictory. However, DBT teaches us that both goals can be achieved together.

DBT has about six points that work together. As a patient using DBT, you are advised not to think too far into the future because that can trigger episodes such as destructive behaviors, depressive states, suicidal behaviors, and eating disorders.

Instead, individuals are taught healthy and positive ways of dealing with stress and intense emotions, regulating emotions, and improving relationships with loved ones. DBT aims to identify, change, and support individuals so they can cope with unhealthy and negative behaviors and emotions, especially in social situations.

Brief History of DBT

DBT was first founded in the 70s by Marsha Linehan, a suicide researcher at the time. Before then, she didn't know a lot about borderline personality disorder (BPD), but she became familiar with it later on. The researcher found the effectiveness of DBT in treating borderline personality disorder. Decades later, BPD practices seem to have become open to argument since DBT is now being used to treat many other mental health issues.

Linehan engaged her patients with real-world examples instead of having one-way conversations with them to get the desired responses. She succeeded in teaching her patients to react differently when in various situations. The process Linehan used removes the challenges that had been confusing therapists who were treating suicidal patients. Studies have revealed DBT as effective in treating self-injurious behavior and suicidal attempts. DBT is also used in treating drug and alcohol addiction. This therapy has shown positive results in patients within these groups. It is now a widely recognized and accepted form of therapy in different parts of the world.

DBT vs. CBT

Perhaps you've heard about CBT before, and at one point you've confused it to mean the same thing as DBT. Well, DBT is a form of CBT that differs in terms of skills.

With DBT, there is the addition of acceptance, mindfulness techniques, and no form of judgment. DBT eliminates the judgmental properties of CBT to ensure that the way an individual thinks isn't seen as wrong, distorted, or erroneous. The goal is to help individuals change how they think.

DBT acknowledges that a problem exists with how an individual thinks while encouraging them to accept this truth without judgment. This helps them seek ways to change their thinking to make it more healthy and balanced.

The model of DBT also shows that it's quite different from CBT. While DBT is a principle-driven therapy, CBT is more of a protocol-based therapy. There are principles guiding DBT that allow flexibility for the therapist, whereas CBT follows stricter procedures. For example, when an individual has a panic attack, only certain rules are followed for the treatment, including abdominal breathing and psychoeducation. This isn't the case for DBT because it allows added flexibility.

Another difference between the two therapies is how the treatments are delivered. DBT has four modes of therapy: skills group, individual therapy, therapy team, and telephone consultation. CBT is provided in an individual format or a group session, and the two rarely occur simultaneously.

While both CBT and DBT incorporate self-monitoring, it is taken to a different level in DBT by using behavior tracking sheets. DBT also differs in the way the sessions are structured to address behavior and in how the stages of the treatment are determined by the threat and severity of the target behaviors.

The DBT Model

DBT consists of four main modules. However, my professional experience has shown me that DBT can be provided to clients effectively without including all the modules. Therefore, research on DBT for BPD acknowledges the complete model, including individual therapy, skills training groups, telephone consultation, and the consultation team.

Individual Therapy

Here, clients attend individual sessions with a therapist weekly. This individual therapy aims to help individuals utilize the skills they've learned in the group to reduce behaviors such as self-harm, suicide, and use of a substance. The individual session has a clear format and session.

Skills Training Group

This psychoeducational, structured group format aims to develop and improve an individual's capabilities. The skills training group is divided into four modules. They include interpersonal effectiveness skills, emotional regulation skills, distress tolerance skills, and core mindfulness skills.

Interpersonal effectiveness skills: These skills aim to help clients reduce the interpersonal chaos that is often present in their lives and is primarily about how to be more assertive. Clients are taught to think about what they most want to get out of interaction (for example, if they have a specific objective, if they wish to keep or even improve the relationship, or if they wish to keep or improve their self-respect), and then they are taught skills that will make it more likely for them to reach this goal.

Core mindfulness skills: In 1993, Linehan broke down the concept of mindfulness into smaller parts to ensure individuals could understand it and can easily incorporate it into their lives. Mindfulness was formerly used to treat BPD by reducing the confused perception of one's self. However, mindfulness has proven to be helpful in many more ways now. When individuals have increased awareness, they are aware of their emotions, thoughts, and urges.

Individuals can learn the skills of attempting to manage emotions efficiently and tolerating the emotions they can't do anything about. They will understand that they don't need to act on internal experience, but that a simple acknowledgment of the experiences will ensure they dissipate gradually.

Emotional regulation skills: The goal of emotional regulation skills is to reduce mood liability. Individuals are made to understand the workings of their emotions and other details such as why they need their emotions and why they shouldn't get rid of them even when they are very discomforting and painful. Individuals will also learn the connection between feelings, thoughts, and behaviors and understand that changing one of these will affect the others. In this module, self-validation and other skills to help individuals manage their emotions more effectively are emphasized.

Distress tolerance skills: The distress tolerance skills are also called the crisis survival skills. This module aims to help individuals survive crises without engaging in unhealthy behaviors such as self-harm, suicide attempts, and substance abuse. The skills will help individuals soothe and distract themselves from the issue instead of dwelling on it, since brooding on it will make them act on their urges and bring about painful emotions.

While these skills can be taught in individual therapy, they are addressed in a group format for several reasons. First, individuals with difficulty regulating their emotions often move from one crisis to another, making it extremely difficult to teach skills in an individual session when they need help with their current crisis. Validation is also an important aspect; individuals benefit from being in the same group as others with similar problems.

Learning can be more effective with group therapy since individuals learn from the experiences of other group members. In addition, since interpersonal issues surface in the group, it can be a great opportunity to practice the learned skills and allow individuals to receive coaching on how to use the skills to act more appropriately.

Telephone Consultation

This medium is used to coach individuals on using skills they've been taught. Telephone consultation is a brief interaction that aims at helping clients identify the skills that are more helpful in certain situations and how to overcome obstacles while using the skills effectively.

Consultation Team

Linehan has made it clear that DBT is incomplete without a team. The composition of a consultation team varies depending on the environment. Generally, the team consists of the therapists in a DBT clinic including psychologists, social workers, psychiatrists, and others working in the training group.

This is a straightforward process for therapists working in a clinical setting. However, it can be complicated for those working in private practice. The reason is simple! The team is needed to ensure therapists are on track with their practice. Therefore, therapists in private practice may need to form a team that consists of other private DBT therapists around them while ensuring that confidentiality is strictly adhered to.

As a practitioner in private practice, I am fortunate to have psychiatrists working in a DBT clinic to support me with consultations. The team size doesn't matter;

what's important is that the therapist receives objective feedback about their practice.

The DBT consultation team is used in two ways: providing support to therapists by pushing them to develop their skills in using the DBT model and coordinating case discussion. The team must ensure that the therapist adheres to DBT strategies and techniques in case discussion. They are also in charge of addressing feelings of burnout.

The team also uses DBT techniques such as being nonjudgmental and taking a dialectal stance to prevent other team members from getting roped into power struggles that can disrupt the therapeutic process.

Exercise: Reason for Change

Before moving to the next section, now is a good time to think about your reason for reading this book. First, you need to identify those changes you want to make. So, in this exercise, you will write down three ways your child reacts to certain emotions—reactions you would want to change. This way, you become committed to replacing those behaviors with better ways of coping.

Write down three damaging things your child does when angry, anxious, or overwhelmed.

- --

- --

So, how could a better understanding of the things you have mentioned help you? Will it contribute to a better parenting experience?

- --

- --

- --

DBT skills and strategies can help you reduce the intensity of emotional waves and balance your emotions when they overwhelm you. We'll discuss that later.

Emotional Intensity and Your Child's Feelings

Does your teen throw tantrums and show displeasure by complaining or pouting? Do their demands become so relentless that you feel you have no other choice but to give in? Do you always wonder why your child is mostly emotional and tends to react intensely to situations that should've been ignored? Does it take very long for them to get over things?

Like adults, teens have emotions too. Their emotions are very real and not easily ignored. How you feel affects what you do, how you do it, and your perception of yourself. Knowing this makes understanding your child's intense behavioral responses important. Unfortunately, these are emotions they find hard to manage.

The following section will explain the driving force behind your child's behaviors and your reactions to those behaviors. Knowing this will position you in a good place to use the skills and strategies we'll be discussing in this book.

Primary and Secondary Emotions

Everyone (babies, teens, and adults) has primary and secondary emotions. While the primary emotions are based on biology and are almost automatic, the secondary emotions are created by reactions to primary emotions.

You don't have much control over your primary emotions, but you have a bit of control over the creation and perpetuation of secondary emotions. Your secondary emotions last longer than the primary ones, leading to more maladaptive behavioral responses.

Let's quickly look at how primary emotions happen and secondary emotions are created.

Primary Emotions Happen

Primary emotions include anger, fear, sadness, joy, disgust, and surprise. These emotions are usually hard-wired in you. They are your first reaction and the emotions you feel when a situation affects you. You experience them physiologically as they come and go like waves on the shore.

Exercise: Primary Emotions

This exercise aims to help you understand primary emotions by looking at a situation that will likely make you experience primary emotions.

Imagine being called to your child's school by the principal. You don't have significant details, but it seems like your child got into a fight. While driving to school, you think about the situation.

What are those feelings you'd have while driving?

Secondary Emotions Are Created

Let's look at the example of being called by the principal of your child's school. You've listed the primary emotions you felt after hearing the news in the preceding exercise. The primary emotions may be fear, alarm, and anger, especially if this is not the first time hearing that your child got into a fight.

On arriving at the principal's office, you are informed that your child got hit by a classmate, and he wasn't the instigator. This makes you start thinking about the initial anger you felt and how you've erroneously jumped to conclusions. Your current thought will create a secondary emotion in you, which will likely be guilt.

Your secondary emotions are your reactions to your primary emotions. They are also the result of the assumptions and beliefs you learned throughout your life. For example, if during your younger years your parents showed disappointment when you felt a fit of unjustified anger, you may experience guilt whenever you feel anger. You can have many secondary emotions in response to one primary emotion; however, it might be so much and so overwhelming that you won't remember the primary emotions that triggered them.

Your Thoughts, Feelings, and Behaviors

No emotion occurs in isolation. Your emotions are a result of cognitive processes and physiological reactions. It's either something internal, which can be your thought, or something external, which can be an event that makes you experience an emotion. The emotions may pop up so quickly that you aren't even aware of the trigger/cause.

Thoughts lead to feelings, which lead to behaviors

Your feelings are directly related to your thoughts, which lead to your behavioral responses. Your thoughts are your internal beliefs, phrases, images, and attitudes. Some of your thoughts may happen so automatically that you aren't aware of their existence. On the other hand, feelings are the physiological reactions you experience that shape your present experience. The result of thoughts and feelings is behavior. Behavior is how you respond and act due to how you feel.

You definitely can't scan your child's head to know exactly what they think. You can see only their behaviors resulting from their feelings and thoughts. Since you aren't 100% certain of the feelings and thoughts behind the behavior, you will likely make some assumptions. Depending on different factors, your assumptions may either be accurate or not. Your child's reality and your assumptions may be totally different. As a result, your child may find it difficult to express themselves and share exactly how they are feeling or why they are feeling it. We'll be discussing this later in this book, where you'll learn ways to help your child be more vocal in telling you how they feel.

To understand the connection between thoughts, feelings, and behaviors, let's quickly look at an example below, which describes how different thoughts about the same event can lead to different behaviors and feelings.

When your child isn't doing what you want them to do (event), you start thinking:

"Why do my words always fall on deaf ears? Why must we always go through this anytime he needs to do something?" You may get angry (your feeling) and lash out (your behavior).

Or

"Okay, I will let this slide since he is having a bad day."

In this case, you may feel relieved (your feeling) and get over it (your behavior).

In the example above, what you told yourself about the event (your thoughts) has affected your feelings and behavior.

By being aware of your thoughts, you will have the skills needed to change your behavioral and emotional responses to situations.

On the other hand, regardless of being aware or not, your child also responds to *their* thoughts. The example below will explain how different thoughts can lead to a behavioral and emotional response in a teen.

Your child sees a boy he recognizes (event). Then, he thinks, *"Is the boy ignoring me?"* (thought). Then, he gets sad (emotion) and slowly withdraws from that situation (event).

Or

Perhaps, your child says out loud, *"The boy there is my friend!"* (thought). He is happy (emotion) and approaches the boy to say hello (behavior).

As you can see, what you think about a situation affects how you feel and behave in that instance.

Your child is not their behavior

Behaviors aren't constant; they can be changed. Your child's behavioral responses are usually learned and are not inborn or ingrained in their personalities. Learning about and understanding your child depends on how you separate your child from their behaviors. Your child is not their behavior. Their behaviors are what they do and not who they are.

Your child may be anxious or act angrily by screaming and yelling. This doesn't suggest that they are an angry child. It just shows that your child is someone who screams and yells when angry. Also, you can't say you have a disobedient child just because they failed to follow instructions.

Why is this distinction important, you may ask? No one wants their child to grow up feeling ashamed, damaged, or worried that they have a flawed character. You want your child to know that they are not their behaviors. You want them to feel loved and accepted despite their feelings and behaviors. If you want a child who will grow up with a positive image, you need to teach them that their behavior only defines what they do and not who they are.

Exercise: A Story of Emotion

This exercise aims to walk you through your *story of emotions*. For now, you will be learning skills that will help you change your response to situations, since having awareness is essential. However, as you continue reading this book and learning skills, your stories may change.

The first task is to recall a recent situation that stirred up negative emotions in you and write down a brief description of the situation.

_____

_____

_____

_____

The next task is to consider the questions below and write down your answers. While writing, notice where you've made changes.

Your risk factors and vulnerabilities:

Describe how you feel before the event occurs.

_____

_____

_____

_____

_____

_____

_____

<u>Your trigger</u>:

What happened?

<u>Your beliefs and thoughts</u>:

What are your thoughts about what happened? What did you have to say after the event?

Responses and body sensations:

How exactly did your body feel?

_____

_____

_____

_____

_____

Name your emotion:

What name can you use to describe what you felt?

_____

_____

_____

_____

_____

Your actions and behaviors:

What was your reaction like as a result of how you felt? What response would've been better?

When you understand the story of your emotions, it puts you in a better place for self-awareness and changing how you interact with your child. But, of course, your child has their unique stories of emotions affecting how *they* feel or behave.

Life is already hard enough, and we aren't oblivious to that fact. But in this case, you aren't stuck or helpless in this tussle with your emotions. If you can do the work to implement the skills and strategies of DBT, your reactions to intense emotions will change, and you can make the same changes in your child.

The reason is simple. Regardless of genetics, DBT skills can influence the outcome of all anger and conflict, and they can alter the state of your relationship. Therefore, there is hope if you continue reading this book. What's in this book has changed the lives of many (for the better); it will change yours too.

CHAPTER 2:

EMOTION DYSREGULATION IN TEENS: A PHASE OR A PROBLEM?

Many parents think they are fully prepared for anything in their teenager's life because they've experienced both the "terrible twos" and the "extreme eights." However, parenting becomes a big deal when your child hits their teenage years. During this period, you can easily feel overwhelmed in managing the effects of puberty hormones, general teen angst, and social media influence.

Some teens even start acting in ways you can't recognize. In fact, many teenagers experience emotional dysregulation, a mental health symptom. Therefore, as parents, you need to know what to look for and how to seek help for your teen.

Parents experience the direct and experiential awareness of the unstable emotional lives of their children. Since you were once a teen and have experienced adolescence yourself, you should have an idea of what the emotional life of a teenager is like.

How exactly was your emotional life then? Was it rocky? Smooth? Did you have it all together or sometimes allow your emotions to get better of you?

I am guessing you experienced a combination of the above. Sometimes you experienced good days, while at other times it wasn't that great. But, regardless of their experience, most teens have experienced various kinds of days; even days when their emotions were all over the place and days that seemed like the worst time of their lives. And some days can also feel like the best they've ever had.

Now, I want you to look back and understand that the rollercoaster of emotions you've experienced in the past is part of your growth; it's your learning phase. I want you to empathize with your teen now and forgive them for their attitudes, impulsive behaviors, and moods. These expressions summarize how teenagers feel and look from the outside.

Of course, your teen is like that for a good reason. Their developing brains form from two directions simultaneously—top-down and bottom-up. The top part is the newest part of the brain, which generates logical thoughts, modulates emotions, regulates impulses, and weighs risk and reward. The bottom part, which is the oldest part of the brain, generates emotions and unconscious reactions.

To better understand whether emotional dysregulation is just a phase in a teen's life or if it is likely to pose a problem, let's start with discussing what emotional dysregulation means.

Understanding Emotional Dysregulation

The team at Rogers Behavioral Health suggests that people experience emotions differently, and some people experience emotions more intensely than others. People with intense emotions experience mood shifts with feelings that linger longer. However, when they find it hard to cope with their intense feelings, this will lead to emotional dysregulation.

But what is emotional dysregulation?

Emotional dysregulation is the inability to stay psychologically and emotionally balanced, resulting in counterproductive and maladaptive behavior. According to Clearview Women's Center for Mental Health, emotional dysregulation affects almost 3% of people in the United States. These people have difficulty managing their emotional responses, making them seem aggressive and conflict-driven.

Emotional dysregulation is more of a symptom than a disorder. Someone experiencing it can feel emotions more intensely than they should and might feel them for a longer period. As a result, they experience these emotions at inappropriate times and respond to them extremely. The common sign of it is extremely emotional instability and severe mood swings.

People who are more likely to experience emotional dysregulation are people with mood disorders and personality disorders. However, it's not limited to these people alone; it exists in other scenarios. For example, people with ADHD can experience emotional dysregulation even if it's not present all the time. Also, those with anxiety disorders or who are manic-depressive can experience emotional dysregulation.

As mentioned earlier, emotional dysregulation isn't so much a disorder as, rather, a symptom of something bigger.

One of the main causes of emotional dysregulation is childhood trauma, despite what the diagnosis usually suggests — anxiety, depression, PTSD, ADHD, and Schizoaffective Disorder. According to research, if you could properly trace it back, you'd find that there was trauma at some point in your teen's childhood.

But why and how does trauma cause emotional dysregulation? What does emotional dysregulation look like in teens? Can it become a problem? Is it okay to just live with it or must it be treated?

When a child experiences trauma, which can be as mild as minimal neglect or as severe as physical abuse, the brain gets affected. It's either that the brain's neural pathways don't form or they become damaged, preventing messages from getting to where they need to reach in the brain. As a result, the prefrontal cortex can be damaged by the trauma. The prefrontal cortex controls decision-making and emotional regulation, so imagine how it would feel if it's been damaged.

When the prefrontal cortex is underdeveloped or damaged, it becomes difficult to behave appropriately. Also, when the brain is in a survival mode much of the time, stress hormones and adrenaline will be released frequently into the body, causing different biological and neurological issues for teens.

Emotional dysregulation in teens may look like this:

It's important to know that puberty seems to exacerbate the signs of emotional dysregulation in teens. They struggle with managing their emotions because of the pool of hormones rushing through their bodies. They get so angry that they can ruin all the relationships they have.

Teens may experience extreme anger that doesn't come with a justifiable reason. They may cry excessively for a longer time and more intensely. They may become physically aggressive to other people and themselves too. They may experience bouts of impulsivity, resulting in harmful risk-taking such as suicidal ideation at an early age, and they may become overly fearful of what's in their future. Sometimes, there is a quick movement between the opposite ends of their emotional spectrum. For example, they may be elated one moment and feel depressed a few moments later. They experience extreme impulsivity and make poor choices without giving the options much thought.

Teens with emotional dysregulation struggle to integrate socially with their environment because their emotions run wild. Even when they try to integrate socially, they can't sustain it for long. They usually have trouble in school and get into fights easily.

Emotional dysregulation entails the extreme side of not being able to manage emotions.

While it's possible to live without treating emotional dysregulation, it can be challenging and threatening to some teenagers. According to a study published in the *Journal of Youth and Adolescence,* the inability to regulate emotions, and the trauma of experiencing them extremely, have caused an increase in suicide rates. Emotional dysregulation can completely disrupt your child's ability to live in a healthy way.

The treatment for this symptom varies; therapy and medications are usually the go-to options. However, using medication for teens can be complicated due to concerns for their developing brains. In addition, some medications can affect the brain, defeating the essence of the treatment.

Usually, teens with emotional dysregulation are treated with therapeutic interventions and environmental changes before medication is considered. These environmental changes could be in the form of modifications in the school environment, for example.

Note that no matter the treatment your teen is receiving to keep their emotions in check, this is a problem that should be closely monitored to ensure they are safe.

Don't be weary; there is hope for your child. There is hope for them to be in control of their emotions and not be consumed by them. However, it takes you as the parent to be helpful and intentional in this journey.

Exercise: Understanding Emotions

Why do you think you have emotions? Are your emotions good? Has there ever been a time when you cursed at your emotions? Perhaps, you wanted to get rid of them completely. Your emotions are useful for a couple of reasons, and you can change them since an emotion doesn't last forever. However, without understanding the functions of emotions, you can't expect to change them yourself. To further this understanding, answers to the questions below.

Think of a time you misread someone's emotions. What emotion were you able to read from them? Did the misinterpretation affect your interaction?

Do you remember a moment when your expression of emotion was misread? What kind of emotions did you feel? What emotions got misinterpreted? How did it feel to be misread by others?

Can you think of some situations where your emotions prompted you to take action before you could think about it?

Recall a moment when your emotion helped you overcome a challenge in your environment, making it easier to get something done — for example at home, in school, and in the community. Even though it's not a pleasant emotion, it helps you get something done.

What Causes Emotional Dysregulation?

For many years now, there has been ongoing research and debate surrounding the exact cause of emotional dysregulation. However, research indicates that teenagers who have experienced early trauma are more susceptible to developing maladaptive emotional patterns, also known as emotional dysregulation, than those who haven't.

The following are some childhood experiences that can lead to emotional dysregulation:

- Physical abuse
- Emotional abuse
- Sexual abuse and rape
- Physical neglect
- Emotional neglect
- Parental mental illness
- Parental alcohol and substance use
- Caregiver maltreatment
- Loss and grief (such as the death of a loved one)
- Exposure to domestic violence

Two things to note about teens with emotional dysregulation are 1) not every teen who experiences trauma in the early years will develop emotional dysregulation, and 2) the cause of emotional dysregulation isn't limited to what I've listed above. The trauma may result from your teen's environment, including trauma outside the home or neighborhood violence.

Some parents assume they are bad parents, and as a result, their kids have to deal with emotional dysregulation. If you are one of those parents, then you've assumed wrongly. Trauma is rooted in different origins, which may have no connection to parental behavior. However, if your teen is experiencing emotional dysregulation, you can assess yourself for any history of emotional dysregulation, mental illness, and alcohol abuse of your own.

We'll now discuss teenagers and what happens in their developing brains.

Teenagers and Their Developing Brains

During the developmental stage of adolescence, the bottom part of the brain outpaces the top part, and the old part becomes more powerful than the new one. On an individual level, the old part is referred to as old because it's one of the first parts to be developed. It's a limbic system associated with emotions and reward. It is where emotions like pain, pleasure, love, and fear emanate.

On an evolutionary level, the old part of the brain is referred to as that because, according to biology, the old part of the brain, in organisms with a complex brain, is the first to appear.

On the individual level, the new part of the brain is referred to as new because it's the prefrontal cortex, the last section to develop. This part of the brain is associated with complex logical thought, assesses and predicts outcomes according to information received, and prevents counterproductive behaviors. On an evolutionary level, the new part is referred to as that because, according to biology, the prefrontal cortex in an organism with a complex brain is one of the last structures to form.

No animal has a prefrontal cortex like humans. Therefore, when the oldest part of the brain becomes more powerful than the newest part, the resulting behavior may seem chaotic, uncontrolled, and irrational; the teen may act like a child.

When both the new and old parts of the brain start seeking dominance over each other, the teen's behavior may seem both logical and illogical within moments. This type of behavior is what we know as emotional dysregulation; examples of it include impulsivity, moodiness, and irrational behaviors.

In a typical teen behavior, while the emotions win some times, the prefrontal cortex wins other times. When diagnosed clinically, emotional dysregulation means that for different complex reasons, the brain develops regulatory functions that will lead to a mental illness (pathology).

According to evidence, emotional dysregulation in teenagers is associated with and is also a known risk factor for these mental health disorders:

- Anxiety disorders
- Eating disorders
- Depressive disorders
- Bipolar disorder
- Post-traumatic stress disorder (PTSD)
- Borderline personality disorder (BPD)
- Eating disorders
- Substance use disorder (SUD)
- Oppositional defiant disorder (ODD)
- Alcohol use disorder (AUD)
- Disruptive mood dysregulation disorder (DMDD)

Also, emotional dysregulation can be associated with as well as a risk factor for these maladaptive behaviors:

- Risky sexual behavior
- Non-suicidal self-injury (NSSI)
- Suicide attempts (SA)
- Suicidal ideation (SI)

The above behaviors and disorders are quite serious. Therefore, if a mental health specialist diagnoses your child with emotional dysregulation, there is a good chance the professional will suggest expert support and treatment at a psychiatric facility that specializes in handling adolescents with mental health issues.

Exercise: Knowing the Myths of Emotions

The aim is to introduce you to some myths about emotions and write a challenge that makes sense to you. A challenge will be provided—however, try to come up with another challenge for the myth or rewrite the one given.

Myth 1: *Allowing others to know that I feel bad is a sign of weakness.*

The challenge: Allowing others to know that you feel bad is a way to communicate your emotions.

Your challenge:

Myth 2: *There is a particular way to feel in different situations.*

The challenge: We all respond differently to things, so there is no preferred or correct way to feel.

Your challenge:

Myth 3: *My being emotional means that I am out of control.*

The challenge: My being emotional simply shows that I am only human.

Your challenge:

Myth 4: *As the name suggests, negative feelings are bad and can destroy me.*

The challenge: Negative feelings are natural responses that help me understand a situation better.

Your challenge:

Myth 5: *I experience painful emotions due to my bad attitude.*

The challenge: Painful emotions result from natural responses to a situation.

Your challenge:

Myth 6: *Certain emotions are useless.*

The challenge: All emotions indicate how I feel in certain situations. It doesn't mean they are useless as they all help me understand how I feel.

Your challenge:

Myth 7: *If people don't approve of my feelings, I shouldn't be feeling that way.*

The challenge: I have a right to feel how I do, regardless of what others think.

Your challenge:

Myth 8: *Others are the best judge of my feelings.*

The challenge: I should be the best judge of how I feel, as others can only guess.

Your challenge:

Myth 9: *My painful emotions should be ignored because they are unimportant.*

The challenge: My painful emotions can be warning signs indicating that a certain situation isn't good for me.

Your challenge:

Myth 10: *Extreme emotions will get me further than regulating my emotions.*

The challenge: Extreme emotions will only cause trouble for me and others. If emotions are extreme, emotional regulation should be helpful.

Your challenge:

Myth 11: *To be creative, I need intense and out-of-control emotions.*

The challenge: I can be in control of my emotions and still be creative.

Your challenge:

Myth 12: *Trying to change my emotions shows inauthenticity.*

The challenge: Change is inauthentic and is a regular part of life.

Your challenge:

Myth 13: *My emotions are a reflection of who I am.*

The challenge: My emotions can be partly, but not completely, who I am.

Your challenge:

Myth 14: *I can do whatever I feel like doing.*

The challenge: I can't do whatever I want because it might be ineffective.

Your challenge:

Myth 15: *Acting on my emotions is an indication that I am a free individual.*

The challenge: A truly free person has the ability to regulate emotions.

Your challenge:

Myth 16: I should always trust my emotions.

The challenge: Emotions can sometimes be trusted using logic.

Your challenge:

What Next?

Many teens struggle to manage their emotions to some extent. The rapid changes they experience in their physical appearance and the influx of hormones can confuse the brain in different scenarios. However, teens that have already experienced emotional dysregulation as a child will notice an extreme uptick in these difficulties when they hit puberty.

Some teens experiencing emotional dysregulation can be dangerous and self-destructive. They push people away and lash out due to anger, sometimes to the extent of ruining their relationships with friends and family members. They may feel depressed to the point that this impacts their ability to cope in school.

Some of the worst results of your teen's emotional dysregulation may come during their euphoric bouts of happiness. At these moments, it is easy to enter into extreme impulsivity and, as a result, engage in vices such as shoplifting, smoking, picking up a drug habit, driving erratically, and engaging in unprotected sexual activities. In other words, without proper management, emotional dysregulation can have fatal consequences for teens.

Naturally, as parents, we want to help our children as much as we can. But with emotional regulation, it becomes hard to know the best way to help. On the good side, mental health providers approve of DBT as working best for teens dealing with intense emotions. With it, you can track your teen's mood fluctuations. Also, you should write down everything you notice happening before, during, and after a mood shift, especially if it's extreme. That way, you can easily recognize possible triggers or what causes the mood swings.

You can try to validate your teen's emotions as much as possible during moments of extreme emotion. Since they feel no one understands them, the validation will help give your child possible relief. This has a calming effect on your child. Avoid lecturing, arguing, or trying to talk them out of their feelings during these times, because this will only aggravate the issue.

You can talk over the signs of emotional dysregulation you've noticed in your teen with your family doctor or any professional health care provider. A medical doctor will help determine if there is an underlying medical condition. If there is none, you will likely be referred to a psychologist or psychiatrist specializing in adolescents.

The clinical psychiatrist or psychologist will evaluate your teen to determine a possible diagnosis. A mental health provider will often recommend therapy and medication to help relieve the child's symptoms. Also, regular therapy can be suggested to help your teen work through their difficult emotions and learn to regulate and navigate them more effectively.

DBT is a form of therapy tailored for teens with emotional dysregulation. Dr. Marsha Linehan invented this therapy to help people manage disruptive behaviors or emotions when all approaches have failed.

Emotional dysregulation can feel overwhelming and seem scary. However, it is more common than people know. With the right approach, using DBT, your teen will learn how to work through their strong and overwhelming emotions and come out better in the end.

CHAPTER 3:

UNDERSTANDING YOUR CHILD'S EMOTIONS

Adolescence will probably not be complete if a teenager doesn't experience at least one episode of emotional outburst. Even you, a parent, went through extremely emotional moments while in your teenage years. This shows that occasional mood swings and emotional outbursts that occur sporadically are normal and are part of your teenager's growth.

Adolescence is a time of major transition, and this causes teenagers to experience a wide range of powerful and fluctuating emotions. Teenagers are still trying to find and accept their identity and the changes that come with it. You may notice that these emotional fluctuations often put them out of balance. Emotional outbursts are not considered important until they become extreme or constant and interfere with daily life. That may indicate a more serious mental health issue and should be looked into immediately.

Intense Emotions, Anger, and Anxiety in Adolescence: Causes and Contributing Factors

There are many reasons teenagers might experience frequent anger, anxiety, or other intense emotions. Teenagers experience emotional outbursts resulting from some seemingly unimportant things that could later prove to be a big deal. Sometimes, you might be able to discern the reason almost immediately. Other times, neither you nor your child can pinpoint why they react the way they do. These intense emotions could be a result of:

Heredity and family background

Do you know that some emotional disorders run in the family? If a family member, parent, or sibling suffers anxiety or depression, your teenager may likely inherit that. They may pick up your method of handling emotional tension too. For example, if you like venting out and creating tantrums when you are angry, your teenager may react in that same manner when experiencing the same emotions. According to research, young people whose parents fight and argue frequently or are overly involved in their children's lives have a high level of sadness and anxiety.

Toxic relationships

Relationships with toxic parents and peers can significantly impair a teenager's self-esteem, leading to emotional tension. Over-controlling, judgmental, frigid parenting, traumatizing social encounters, and emotional maltreatment increase emotional outbursts. You raise anger, induce anxiety, and contribute to sadness when you don't build a genuine relationship with your teen. The same thing applies to the kind of relationship your child has with their peers.

Medical conditions

Some diseases can produce symptoms related to emotional disorders or worsen their symptoms. For example, illnesses such as heart disease, lung issues, and thyroid problems may make your teen more likely to have emotional outbursts.

Certain medications used to treat these illnesses can increase or reduce anger, anxiety, and depression symptoms. This is why, when you or your teen stop or start taking some medications, you may experience intense emotions like anxiety or depression.

Change

Uncertainty bias has an impact on how a teenager deals with change. When a huge life shift occurs, the brain interprets that as a bad event. This can affect their decision-making process and make them feel more anxious and depressed. Teenagers who have experienced huge changes such as the birth of a new sibling, moving to a new house, or traveling to a different country are more likely to experience emotional outbursts. When teenagers feel uncomfortable in their surroundings, they are prone to experiencing a lot of tension and worry.

Environmental stress

Research studies have proven that environmental factors can also cause anxiety, depression, and anger in teenagers. However, these factors are mostly related to tense situations a teenager has witnessed or experienced. For example, childhood maltreatment, the death of a loved one, being bullied or attacked, and witnessing violence are common triggers for intense emotions.

Sleep deprivation

Lack of sleep can make a teen feel agitated and irritated. It can also affect their weight, memory, attention, and immunity. Your teen requires eight to ten hours of sleep per night to be mentally alert and emotionally balanced. Set a consistent bedtime for your teen and keep television and other gadgets out of their room to encourage healthier sleep. The light from these gadgets does not rest the mind. Instead, it decreases melatonin production and increases the activeness of the mind. They can try listening to music or audiobooks before going to bed instead.

Wrong eating or drinking habits

At this stage of their lives, teenagers are very likely to prefer junk or fast food to healthy food. Junk food could worsen your teen's mood and make them feel overwhelmed and tired. Anxiety disorder also occurs in conjunction with alcohol and substance abuse. Eating healthy food will do your teenager a lot of good. A healthy diet can help boost energy levels and mental sharpness and neutralize the teenager's mood. Make an effort to be a role model for your teen by doing more home cooking, eating more fruits and vegetables, and avoiding junk food and soda. These are all good ideas to improve the eating habits of your teen.

Warning Signs That Your Teen's Emotions Are out of Control

It's natural to have a surge of emotion from time to time. For example, if a teen is required to take an exam or make a significant decision, they may feel worried or nervous. However, intense emotions go beyond the teen's normal feelings of rage and grief. When it affects your teenager's capacity to function, it becomes distressing. In addition, they have little control over how they react in different situations. Therefore, it is advisable to address your teenager's outbursts in the early stages — before they become a habit or coping strategy.

You are probably lost and don't know the signs to look for that indicate your teen is out of control. Unfortunately, you aren't alone. It can be hard for caretakers or parents to know if their teens are just "being teenagers" or if it is something more severe. Some of the behaviors you see, such as mood swings, might be related to typical adolescent behavior and not necessarily point to a problem. Knowing when there are indicators of a more serious problem, on the other hand, can be very useful.

Some warning signs to show that your teen's emotions are out of control include:

Violent, disrespectful, or self-destructive behavior

If there have been episodes where your teenager slams the door in your face, stomps their feet in a fit of rage, or destroys nearby objects after being scolded, know that these are warning signs that teenagers with extreme emotional outbursts display. The teen often disrespects authority figures, throws unnecessary tantrums, and is not ready to listen to corrections. They might start damaging property, stealing, and engaging in fights. Arguments that never seem to end, domestic violence, getting into fights, and running into trouble with the law are warning signs that your teen is going beyond ordinary adolescent rebellion.

Use of hard drugs or alcohol

In a bid to relieve themselves of the emotional tension, some teens resort to the use of hard drugs and alcohol. When drinking or using drugs becomes a habit, especially if trouble at school or home follows from it, this could imply there's an underlying issue. Substance abuse is a risky coping mechanism. It causes the teen to lose sight of the main issue and focus instead on the immediate gratification they get from the drugs. Usage of heavy drugs is never a good sign.

Skipping school or withdrawing from social activities

When teenagers suddenly start to withdraw from participating in school or other social activities, their emotions may be out of control. The teenager might avoid meeting up with friends and dislike the company of others altogether. Going to school feels like stress, and they would rather be alone in bed all day long. A sudden change in their social circle could also be a concern, especially if the new friends support inappropriate behavior. The adolescent might begin to defy sensible rules and boundaries. Similarly, if your teen spends too much time alone, it could be a sign of trouble, so watch closely.

Persistent mood swings and engaging in early sexual activity

When mood swings become persistent and refuse to abate, there might be a problem. Sudden personality changes, declining grades, recurrent sadness, anxiety, or sleep difficulties could be signs of depression or other emotional health problems.

The adolescent may also be heard making sexually-explicit remarks or engaging in sexual activities. Requests to change their behavior will have little effect on them, and they will refuse to change despite the consequences.

When to Get Help for Your Child

If you're worried about your teenager's mental health, your family, friends, and partner may tell you to relax and wait until they grow out of it. This is sometimes sound advice, but that isn't always the case. There are occasions when waiting to get your child help for their mental health difficulties is simply not a good choice. The earlier a child receives treatment for emotional or behavioral issues, the easier it is to help them.

Emotional outbursts that occur regularly for six months or longer may indicate that your teen requires urgent assistance. These outbursts are usually more serious, including violent or disruptive conduct. You know you should get help for your teen when they start exhibiting:

Self-destructive behaviors

If your teen has attempted or threatened suicide or self-harm such as cutting or piercing themselves, you should seek urgent help. In addition, you should look out for the teenager's interaction with friends and classmates. This is because the teen might be injuring or threatening to injure others. Seek professional help if your child makes threats, fights, breaks things, injures themselves and others, or shows other aggressive behaviors.

Sit down with your child and try to talk to them the first time it happens. Try to figure out what's going on. Then, you'll need to teach your teen how to express their needs and the seriousness of their needs in a different, decent way.

Self-destructive acts could be their way of seeking attention. You could, however, teach them a more healthy way of demonstrating what they want. In this manner, whatever problems they have, you might be able to work together to solve them.

Sleep or eating disorders

If you notice a huge difference in your teen's sleeping or eating pattern, get help as soon as possible. An eating disorder often comes from using food to distract themselves or cope with an issue. The eating disorder should be addressed if a teen experiences rapid weight loss or gain, changes in shape, or feelings of dissatisfaction with body shape and size.

The teenager might also sleep in irregular patterns or lose sleep altogether. If there is a notable difference in your teen's sleep pattern, then this might be an indicator of an emotional issue. Seek the help of a professional. You could also encourage the teen to sleep by creating a bedtime routine to facilitate sleep. For example, have the teen decorate their room according to their preferences. They may control the amount of light and temperature in the room to help them sleep better. It may also be beneficial to pay greater attention to what they eat before bedtime.

Withdrawal from people and activities

If your teen suddenly begins to lose interest in the people or activities that used to thrill them, then you might need to seek help for them. Some emotional outbursts take the pleasure away from activities that were once enjoyable. Keep an eye out for your child's canceling plans or making up reasons to avoid doing things they used to enjoy.

Once you notice the continuous occurrence of these types of behaviors, an immediate measure is to request that your child go out with friends rather than lie in a dark room all day. Keep them occupied and engage them in fun activities to keep them around friends and family.

It is necessary to get help if your teenager's behavior is causing persistent problems at school or significantly disturbing your family life. You should also seek help if the teenager suddenly starts performing poorly in school and threatens to run away.

5 Strategies for Managing Your Child's Emotions

Parents are emotionally attached to their children. No parent can easily sit by and watch their teen wallow in self-pity and emotional derailment. It's difficult to watch your adolescent draw away from you, but patience and consistency are key in situations like these. Just because you have sought professional assistance, your work is not finished. You still have core roles to play as a parent. I can't promise that you won't get frustrated along the way. I can only guarantee that the following strategies will make things easier for you and your teen.

1. Give some time off

Do not follow your teen around, demanding apologies, while they are still enraged. This will simply prolong or exacerbate the fury. It may even result in a physical response. Instead, let your teen take a short time-out or ask for permission to leave the room for a moment of privacy. This should be done whenever they need to calm themselves down. Make it clear to your teenager that this is something they should do before they are tempted to misbehave.

Exercise: Assumptions Practice

Linehan gave several assumptions to guide the therapeutic work of DBT so it can be accepted as fact. These assumptions, including the ones developed by psychologist Alec Miller, are helpful for the parents of teens with intense emotions. They want you to accept these assumptions as an integral part of the DBT learning process. They include:

- There is no absolute truth
- The child is doing the best they can
- Your child wants to act differently and make things better
- Your child needs to try harder, do better, and be motivated to change

- Your child should learn new behaviors for important situations in their life
- Family members shouldn't assume the worst, but take things in a more well-meaning way

Examine these assumptions and think of how treating them as facts can change how you feel, think, and act. Then, answer the following questions.

Which assumption can help you the most, and why?

Which assumption challenges you the most, and why?

Recall a time when believing an assumption would have changed how you felt or what you did in the situation. Answering the questions below will help you clarify your thoughts:

Describe the details of the situation. For example, what was your child doing? How were they feeling?

What assumptions would you use? Check the list of assumptions.

_____

_____

Highlight a possible new response. For example, "I walked away and did not argue."

_____

_____

_____

_____

_____

What do you think would be the result of the new response? For example — feeling calmer, yelling less, and experiencing no outbursts.

_____

_____

_____

_____

_____

2. Validate and relate to your teen's feelings

Once your teen is calm, explain that there's nothing wrong with feeling angry. Still, there are unacceptable methods of expressing it. Some parents may unknowingly diminish a child's feelings, which is the wrong approach. Don't say things like "stay quiet" or "stop overreacting." If you say any of these things to your child, you're teaching them that their emotions are invalid. Instead, let them know that their feelings are valid even if they appear out of proportion at the moment.

That extra element of validation communicates to your child that everyone experiences such emotions at some point in their lives. At the same time, teach your youngster that emotions are transient, and the way they are feeling right now will last only a few minutes.

Even if you don't understand why your teen acts the way they do, letting them know you understand they're going through intense feelings may help. Let your teen understand that crying, feeling upset, and being irritated are not terrible things, nor are they marks of weakness for teenagers.

Exercise: Validation Practice

The steps below will help you practice validating your child. Read it repeatedly and always refer to it when facing a challenging situation or when you want to evaluate an interaction that you could've handled better. Practicing this exercise is important.

Step 1: Acting Wisely

You will stop, take a step back, observe, and think about the situation here.

- Take a moment before you respond
- Observe the situation you are in
- Identify the things you need to do to help slow down your reaction. For example — closing your eyes for a few seconds, taking a few deep breaths, and unclenching your fists
- Determine your goals
- Don't react emotionally — respond wisely

Step 2: Looking at your child with new eyes

This entails being aware of old patterns and developing new ways of thinking.

- Know that your child is doing the best they can under certain circumstances. Say this to yourself as a reminder.
- Think of what may be contributing to the present behavior.
- Help your child to think about what is going on. For example, is the present situation triggering difficult memories?

Step 3: Exploring what's getting in the way

Consider the possible circumstances impeding the validation of your child.

- What are the concerns or vulnerabilities you bring to the situation?
- Be aware of your feelings and thoughts concerning the situation.
- Has the event triggered old feelings or memories in you?
- Are you judging yourself or your child at this moment?

Step 4: Making a validating statement

It would help if you learned how to make statements that can help calm you and your child, showing your acceptance and understanding of them. It might not be easy at first, but with constant practice, you will find ways that work. Ensure your attempts are genuine.

3. Discuss healthy ways to relieve emotional tension

Many teenagers have outbursts because they don't know how to express themselves. When your teen is relaxed and not having a screaming fit, make some recommendations for better outlets. They need to understand that throwing items, cursing at others, or becoming physically aggressive are unacceptable reactions.

Let them know that if they do these things, there will be consequences.

Suggest healthy and decent ways to relieve their emotional tension. For example, practicing mindfulness, counting, listening to music, writing in a journal, painting, or engaging in a physical activity like walking or cleaning can help teenagers feel better.

Exercise: Being Mindful

Have them write their name slowly and notice how they hold the pen, rotating it into a comfortable position in their hand.

See how differently their name looks when they slow down to mindfully notice what they are doing.

Was it hard or easy for your child to do?

Notice that when they slow down their responses and focus more on their awareness, they can change their automatic response.

4. Identify mood boosters

Discuss with your teenager what they enjoy doing when they are happy. For example, they could enjoy playing a game, reading a comic book, or playing karaoke. Tell them that these activities are their "mood boosters," and they should write them down.

Encourage them to deal with their emotions by doing one of these activities when they are upset or sad.

Exercise: Boost Mood with the Six Senses

Vision: Let them go to their favorite place and take special note of the sights. For example, they can notice the people, colors, shapes, and sizes of things.

Smell: They should use their favorite body wash and aftershave, smell freshly brewed coffee, make popcorn or cookies, and take in the scent of fresh roses from the garden.

Hearing: They should listen to their favorite music repeatedly and pay attention to the sound coming from a musical instrument as well as the sounds of nature (thunder, rain, and birds chirping).

Taste: As they drink their favorite non-alcoholic beverage and eat their favorite foods, encourage them to do it mindfully.

Touch: They can try petting the cat or dog, brushing their hair, taking a long bath, hugging, changing into their most comfortable clothes, and putting a wet cloth on their forehead.

Movement: Suggest going for a walk together, exercising, dancing, and doing yoga.

5. Offer rewards

How you react to your teen's behavior immediately after it occurs determines whether or not the behavior will happen again. You can use rewards to encourage your teen to do the things you want. The best rewards are those that are given immediately after a behavior is exhibited. Both you and your teen will feel good when they act accordingly—you're happy because your teenager has accomplished something you like, and your teen is ecstatic as well since he is receiving something in return.

If you reward your teen with a special gift for pulling themselves together, they may learn to anticipate the gift that comes with controlling their emotions. While it's great to provide rewards, don't go overboard. You don't want your adolescent to learn that becoming upset is the easiest way to acquire your attention or get a gift from you.

Teenagers can be quite difficult to manage; it becomes even more difficult when they have emotional outbursts. Parents want the best for their teens, so they treat them in ways they think are best. You may be correct in some cases, but you may also be the source of your teen's outburst.

It's important to recognize that your child is growing and has outgrown the "baby" stage. Allow the child to choose what they want, but be present to guide and discipline them in a caring manner. Most times, forcing teenagers to do what you want them to do doesn't end well.

Teenagers may find it difficult to cope with emotions. Ensure that your teenager understands that you accept them for who they are. Be empathic and indicate that you genuinely care.

If your teen experiences anxiety or another emotional disorder that interferes with their normal activities, seek professional help. It is important to remember that your teen's emotional troubles aren't an indication that you've failed as a parent. Focus on your teen's current needs rather than assigning blame.

CHAPTER 4:
THE ROAD TO EFFECTIVE PARENTING

Parenting a teen with frequent emotional outbursts will unveil sides of you that you never knew existed. You might become as tensed up as your child and lose your cool at some point.

As parents, the way you react to your teen's emotional outbursts has a huge impact on them. Parenting a teen with frequent emotional outbursts can be difficult and overwhelming. It can sometimes force you to examine their actions and personal limits. Unfortunately, parents can unknowingly promote emotional outbursts in their children by becoming irritable and making offensive statements. This strategy has never been successful in controlling emotional outbursts.

The best way to control your child's outbursts is to try effective parenting. As you strive toward establishing a positive connection and raising a healthy, successful adult, it's critical to allow yourself to make errors and learn alongside your teen. Just keep in mind that the more effective you are as a parent, the "healthier" your adolescent will be.

What Is Effective Parenting?

Effective parenting goes beyond the regular type of parenting that simply provides food and shelter for the teen. It entails a deeper and more dedicated relationship with the child. Effective parenting is the ability of parents to interact and engage with their teens in encouraging them to learn and develop into responsible individuals. It is built on the principles of respect, discipline, boundaries, encouragement, and a variety of training and teaching possibilities. Effective parenting focuses on holding your teen accountable for their actions and helping them develop better problem-solving abilities.

Why Is Effective Parenting Good?

Effective parenting sets the tone for a child's personality, life choices, and overall behavior. It can impact their social, physical, and mental well-being. Teens who have a safe and healthy attachment to their parents are more likely to have happy and fulfilled relationships later in life.

Effective parenting teaches teens how to manage their emotions in stressful and tough situations. Socially, a child raised by parents who use effective parenting will be positive and confident. They raise children who have a better knowledge of the world and what is required of them as teenagers. They talk about the rules with their teens and make sure they understand what's expected of them. They also make certain there are consequences for their actions, regardless of how they feel.

Responding to Your Child's Feelings and Behaviors — Emotionally, Reasonably, and Wisely

The fury of a teenager can make parents uneasy. As a result, you could try to satisfy your teen by giving in to their demands or avoiding particular circumstances to alleviate their anger or unhappiness. Some parents also use intimidation or punishment to stop the rage. In other words, they become irritated and annoyed by their child's rage.

Your teen will, without a doubt, encounter situations that cause emotional outbursts. You can't stop the triggers from happening, but you can show your child the tools for understanding their feelings and teach them how to cope with these feelings healthily and reasonably. Your reaction to your teen's outburst will also influence whether or not your child reacts appropriately. Some parents react emotionally, some reasonably, and others wisely.

Reacting emotionally

Most likely, you're reacting emotionally if you parent primarily with irritation and wrath. However, if you have a short temper and react by yelling, this too is reacting emotionally to your teen's outbursts.

Reacting emotionally does more harm than good. When you are emotional, it is more difficult for you to solve problems, and making plans may seem impossible. You rant, complain, and yell, and the atmosphere becomes tense for both your teen and you. This has not solved any issue; it has simply made the situation worse.

Reacting reasonably

A parent who responds rationally most of the time may be unaware of how emotions affect others. This kind of parent rarely allows emotions to influence their decision-making. They feel calm and unaffected by the emotional outbursts that surround them. The parent will resolve most issues and feel highly confident in their ability to solve problems. On the other hand, they will be uncomfortable with emotions and unable to comprehend the feelings of teens or others. They may come off as too strict. Their teens may also dread having a relationship with them if they are sure to become greatly agitated when the problems have no immediate solutions. A father who reacts reasonably and calmly will frequently get annoyed with a mother who operates emotionally and vice versa.

Reacting wisely

Both of these reasonable and emotional parenting styles must be fused to make effective parenting possible. When a parent thinks emotionally, they are unlikely to think rationally or logically. Similarly, a rational parent will have trouble infusing emotions into their decisions or actions and may not recognize the emotions of others. When you react to situations wisely, you will handle your reactions intuitively, and there will be balance in them. You will be able to view the whole picture and use both emotion and logic in making your decision. A wise mind will make you feel more relaxed when making decisions. Reacting wisely will assist you in making the required adjustments to your reactions so that your child's emotional outbursts can be controlled too. If your child has strong emotions or frequently reacts emotionally, it is important for you to think and react as wisely as possible.

Key Features of Effective Parenting

Focusing on the positive rather than the negative is a foundational principle of effective parenting. This isn't to say you should disregard the negative; it just isn't your priority. It also doesn't mean you should become a liberal parent. Instead, the key features of effective parenting ensure that you can use your position as a parent to positively influence your teen's emotions and reactions. It also helps you react wisely to your teenager's emotional outbursts.

With the three positive parenting approaches listed below, you may effectively teach, train, and instruct your teen on controlling their emotions.

Making observations

Parental observation works best when parents and teenagers have a positive, open, and caring connection. Teens are more likely to talk to their parents if they believe they can trust them and will receive helpful counsel, and if parents are open and ready to listen and talk to them. Teenagers who are content with their parental ties are more likely to follow the rules.

It would help if you tracked how much money your kid spends and how long they stay online. Keep an eye on your teen's emotions and conduct at home and talk about any concerns you have. As often as possible, talk to your teen about how they feel and what they think. Know your teen's circle of friends. Talk to your child about their plans with friends and where they intend to go after school. These observations will assist you in getting to know your child better and detecting any early indicators of emotional disorders. Listening, asking questions, providing support and appreciation, and remaining involved in your child's life are ways to parent your teen effectively.

Encouraging, not praising

Encouragement and praise are not the same things. The difference between encouragement and praise is that encouragement recognizes effort, the process, and the celebration of progress. On the other hand, praise is a judgment and is about offering a teenager your approval for their activities. Praise instills a sense of reliance on the opinion of others, while encouragement emphasizes one's efforts and abilities.

Encouragement is more helpful than praise in boosting a child's self-esteem. Overuse of praise can reduce self-esteem in youngsters, making them more competitive and less cooperative.

Encouragement can be a very effective motivator. For example, instead of saying, "You're so calm now," say, "It's so nice that you've been able to work on your emotions." You encourage your child to keep behaving responsibly and positively by noticing and commenting on their responsible decisions and behaviors.

Discipline to teach, not to punish

Do not mistake appropriate parenting for the absence of unpleasant consequences. Effective parenting is not the same as allowing your child to do anything they want or as a "weak" attitude that allows your teen to get away with anything. There is still a place for discipline when parenting teens with emotional outbursts. The problem is that parents discipline their teens out of frustration. The punishment they give is meant to cause pain and not make the child understand that their reaction was wrong.

Your teen may occasionally act in ways that push your boundaries or violate the rules you've established. Outlining the consequences is an approach to dealing with this. If you can make the punishment correct the wrongdoing, your teen will be more likely to learn from the experience. For example, if your child breaks a plate in a fit of rage, a suitable punishment might be to have to replace it himself. This method seeks to assist your teen in understanding your point of view and learning that they must give and take to be successful. If they can benefit from doing the right thing, they should also face the repercussions of doing the wrong thing.

Parenting Strategies for a Child with Intense Emotions

1. Be a role model

Teens are wired to mimic, understand, and absorb the actions of others into their actions. Just like small children, they pay close attention to everything their parents do. Your teen will observe how you handle difficult situations.

How does your teenager perceive your dealings with their difficulties and coping mechanisms? Take time to walk the walk. Telling your child what you want them to do isn't enough; showing them is the best method of teaching them. Some of your emotional buttons may be pushed by your child's rage. If you're not conscious of your problems, you may react in ways that are harmful to your child. You could give in to their demands or yell back, but neither of these options will solve the problem. Take a deep breath if you find yourself experiencing strong emotions.

Be the person you want your teen to be, respect them, model positive conduct and attitudes, show empathy for their feelings, and your kid will follow suit. You can advise your teen on how to behave and give them various solutions. Still, if you're mishandling your own emotions (yelling, screaming, or doing something else that isn't positive), your conduct will take precedence over whatever you're advising them to do. You must try to control your outbursts. Then let your teen watch you work through it so they can learn from you.

Exercise: Use the PLEASE Skills

PL: Treat PhysicaL illnesses in your body. Take care of yourself and see a doctor when necessary. Always take the prescribed medication.

E: Balance your Eating by not eating too little or too much. Eat mindfully and avoid foods that make you emotional.

A: Avoid mood-altering substances, alcohol, and drugs.

S: Balance your Sleep. Ensure you get seven to nine hours of sleep every night; it will help to make you feel good. See a doctor if you have sleep disorders.

E: Exercise. Engage in a significant amount of exercise daily. You and your teen should build up to at least twenty minutes of exercise daily.

2. Find out why your teen is sad or upset

Helping your child cope with emotional outbursts will be a lot easier if you know the root cause of the problem. Try to figure out what is causing your adolescent's emotional outbursts. Is your teen stressed out as a result of a major family change? Are they being bullied in school? Do they feel inferior because their classmates have things that they lack? Does your adolescent need someone to listen to who doesn't pass judgment on them? Ask open-ended questions to get the teen to talk about why they're reacting in that way.

Asking questions will be successful only if you have a cordial relationship with your teen. If you and your teen are not on good terms, don't force it. Try to create a relationship by spending time together first. Let your teen open up at their own pace.

Exercise: Identifying What Helps Your Child Feel Better

When they are sad, they feel better when I...

_____

_____

_____

_____

_____

When someone hurts their feelings, they feel better when I...

_____

_____

_____

_____

_____

When they are mad, they feel better when I…

_____

_____

_____

_____

_____

When they are upset, they feel better when I…

_____

_____

_____

3. Problem-solve with your child

If there is a problem, suggesting solutions for your child can be beneficial, but your teen must be a part of the solution and feel like they "own" it. If your teenager believes the solution came from them, they will be more willing to try it. Problem-solving is also an important life skill that your child will improve by practicing. By devoting time and effort to improving your child's problem-solving abilities, you show that you respect their participation in life decisions.

Allowing your kid to figure out how to manage these situations, while assisting them, allows them to learn a difficult but crucial lesson about responsibility. It's critical to provide support and maintain empathy without taking on their troubles or bailing them out. You want your adolescent to understand that they can solve problems and build a sense of cause-and-effect relationships. By being supportive and there for them, you allow teens to understand that they are strong and capable. Ask about what tactics they think would be beneficial to them. With your help, they might be able to come up with some innovative ideas to help them cope with their emotions.

Exercise: Problem Solving to Change Emotions

This exercise involves selecting a promoting event that triggers a painful emotion, selecting an event that can be changed, and turning the event into a problem that needs solving.

Use the questions below to describe the event.

What is the problem? For example, describe the problem by prompting emotions and write down what makes the situation a problem.

Check the facts by looking back and identifying if there is an overreaction. What event triggered the emotion? What are the interpretations or assumptions about the event? Do the emotion and its intensity correlate with the assumption of the situation?

Write down a realistic short-term goal of the problem-solving process. What has happened to show that progress has been made?

It's time to brainstorm solutions. Write down as many of the solutions and coping strategies that come to mind. Don't evaluate them.

---

4. Show love and acceptance

Even though your teenager may feel enraged, unhappy, or anxious, they still require your love and attention. Your role might shift slightly because of their outbursts, but you are still their parent. Even if they claim to despise their parents, they still need the emotional support only parents can give. In addition, they need comfort and self-confidence to deal with peer pressure and other adolescent demands. Teens who lack confidence are more likely to succumb to peer pressure and struggle to uphold wholesome, ethical beliefs.

You're still in charge of keeping them safe; guiding and shaping the kind of adult they will become. They need to know you adore them no matter what and that you are always on their side. You need to show them love and reassure them constantly. Take them on trips, get them gifts, and encourage them. Teens still want your approval and support even when they are kicking and yelling, so try to constantly let them know that you love and accept them the way they are, even if you are dissatisfied or upset yourself.

Exercise: Paying Attention to Positive Events

It's natural for humans to pay more attention to the bad than the good. If you were given eight compliments and one criticism, you will likely ignore the compliments and focus on the criticism. If you've been focusing on the negative aspect of things, it's time to stop and refocus on the positive.

Start doing small positive activities with your teen, and don't let problems ruin the moment. Some of these activities include:

- Watching a movie together
- Having a satisfying, leisurely meal together
- Going for a walk
- Going on picnic dates
- Trying out a new hobby
- Visiting family and friends
- Visiting a zoo or local museum

Even though adding one or two positive activities won't change their lives, it will create happiness, which can add up and make a significant difference over time.

5. Establish boundaries and consequences

While correcting your teen with love, you also have to let them know that they cannot do certain things simply because they are in a fit of rage. At a time when both you and your teen are calm, make them understand that there are inappropriate ways of showing anger. If your teen, for example, destroys the door in a fit of rage, they will have to save money to get it fixed. They will lose some rights if they slam the door in your face.

Boundaries and restrictions are important now more than ever for teenagers; it would help if you established clear limitations and boundaries. Your ability to maintain a level of consistency gets you respect. Make it very clear what is and is not acceptable. It's preferable to have an adolescent who is temporarily enraged than a teen who does not respect you.

Exercise: Let Go of the Emotion, Not the Situation

Letting go of your emotions doesn't suggest letting go of the consequences or situation. It means you are weathering the emotions to become more effective. If you are having an argument with your child and you are angry, let go of the anger until it's dissipated, and then handle the situation more effectively.

You can practice deep breathing to help you maintain calm. To do this:

- Place one of your hands on your chest and the other hand on your abdomen.
- Start inhaling slowly and deeply. Make the air pass through your nose and into your abdomen.

- When you feel at ease with your breathing, inhale through the nose and exhale through the mouth.
- Continue with the slow deep breaths, which should be raising your lower abdomen.
- As you become more relaxed, focus on the feeling and sound of your breath.
- Continue this process for five minutes.

Practice this exercise whenever you feel tense. You can do it anywhere and in any position.

6. Stay connected

Staying engaged and actively listening to what is happening in your teen's life will allow you to more easily understand the triggers for their emotional outbursts. Sometimes the ideal moment for your child to share things with you is during informal, ordinary activities like driving your child somewhere, eating out, or watching TV together.

Parents usually spend more time talking to their teens than interacting with them. Practice paying attention to your children and truly listening to them. You'll be astonished at how much more connected you feel to your child. In addition, you'll probably learn a lot about what they've been thinking and experiencing.

When your adolescent is chatting with you, look at them. Paying attention to what they have to say gives your teenager the message that you value their input. Show that you're interested. Encourage your child to elaborate on what they've said and discuss their thoughts, feelings, expectations, or intentions. Listen without interrupting, judging, or correcting what they are saying. Your goal is to spend time with your child, not to offer advice or assistance until they specifically need it.

Exercise: Describing Your Child in Non-Evaluative Terms

This exercise encourages parents to use descriptive rather than judgmental language with their teens. You can do this by picturing your teenager standing in front of you, then writing down your answers to the following questions.

How does your child look? For example, what's the color of their hair and eyes, and how tall are they? NOTE: Don't use words like skinny or fat because these can be perceived in evaluative ways.

What does your child enjoy doing? What are their hobbies? What's their favorite food? What's their favorite sport?

How does your child spend their day? What grade are they in school? What's their favorite subject? Do they enjoy sports? What sports team are they rooting for?

Does your child have a talent for playing a musical instrument or performing?

You can use many more ways to describe your child than you normally think about. The point is to focus on your child's other qualities rather than just on their emotional intensity. This exercise should help you see your child with new eyes and in new ways.

Finally, managing the emotions of teenagers can be daunting because they are still developing an identity of their own. Effective parenting and reacting wisely will make the job a lot easier. If you take advantage of casual talks during the day, you and your teen will start feeling closer. Think of ways to effectively communicate with your teen and teach them new, acceptable behaviors. Every small conversation is an opportunity to listen to your teen and form bonds with them. Being kind to your teen also helps to foster a cordial relationship. Start saying "please," giving hugs, knocking before entering their bedroom, and cooking their favorite meals. You may have to put your emotions aside once more and think critically.

These activities create a cheerful atmosphere. Even if you don't feel like it, make an effort to be kind to your teen. This sets a good example for your child and demonstrates the importance of spending time together. Teenagers are different—each has their own weaknesses, strengths, and peculiarities. Seek professional help if the strategies you've tried don't give relief, and keep trying. Also, remember that this phase will pass.

FINAL WORDS

You've reached the end of this amazing journey. I must commend you for staying with me to the finish.

The first book of this series, *The DBT Skills Workbook For Teens: Understand Your Emotions and Manage Anxiety, Anger, and Other Negativity to Balance Your Life for the Better*, is also very helpful for your teen. Ensure your teen reads it because it is specifically for teenagers who want to learn skills that help them understand and manage their fluctuating emotions, improve their self-awareness, overcome impulsive behaviors, and effectively deal with relationship issues.

No doubt about it, the teenage years can be quite challenging for any parent. Teenagers may behave recklessly, act notoriously moody, and be unpredictable, making parenting difficult. It's even more difficult for parents with teens who are experiencing emotional dysregulation.

While many teens troubled by anxiety and anger issues require professional treatment to feel better, there are ways parents can help them manage their issues. I hope this book has delivered on its promise of providing effective strategies for managing your teen's intense emotions.

With the right support and guidance, you can help your teen learn new ways to manage their feelings and find more happiness and success in life.

Best Wishes,

The Mentor Bucket

A FREE GIFT TO OUR READERS

What You'll Get:

✓ **11 Essential Life Skills** *Every Teen Need to Learn Before Leaving Home*

✓ *How to* **Be A Calm Parent** *Even When Your Teens Drive You Crazy*

✓ *15 Tips to* **Build Self-Esteem and Confidence** *in Teen Boys & Girls*

Please go to the below URL to download

your FREE gift.

www.thementorbucket.com/gift-dbt-parents

NEXT READ

The DBT SKILLS WORKBOOK FOR TEENS

Understand Your Emotions and Manage Anxiety, Anger, and Other Negativity to Balance Your Life for the Better

Please go to the below URL
for more details.

www.thementorbucket.com/dbt1

DOWNLOADABLE WORKSHEETS

Please go to the below URL to download all worksheets (in pdf format) given in the book.

www.thementorbucket.com/dbt-wsparents.pdf

RECOMMENDED BOOKS

Please go to the below URL and check our recommended books.

www.thementorbucket.com/resources